The Village Pub

When you have lost your inns drown your empty selves,
for you will have lost the last of England

HILAIRE BELLOC

The Village Pub

Roger Protz and Homer Sykes

Weidenfeld and Nicolson
London

This book is dedicated to the memory of George Orwell, whose life and work are a continuing inspiration and whose magnificent 1946 essay 'The Perfect Pub' is an enduring warning to brewery pub 'modernizers'. R.P.

To the most beautiful girl in the world. H.S.

Copyright text © Roger Protz 1992
The moral right of the Author has been asserted.

Copyright photographs © Homer Sykes 1992

First published in 1992 by George Weidenfeld and Nicolson Ltd
Orion House, 5 Upper St Martin's Lane, London WC2H 9EA

British Library Cataloguing-in-Publication Data
A catalogue record for this book is available from the British Library.

ISBN 0–297–83125–9

Designed by Nick Avery
Typeset in Linotron Bembo
at The Spartan Press Ltd,
Lymington, Hants
Printed and bound in Italy

Contents

The First Draught

IN THE BEGINNING ALL INNS OR ALE HOUSES WERE LOCATED IN VILLAGES. Long before the arrival of the Romans, the rural people of the British Isles made alcoholic drinks from honey, apples and pears. Barley and other cereals reached these shores with the sea-going Phoenicians and a type of beer called *curmi* was being made when the Romans marched in with their viniculture. The Romans stuck to wine but introduced the custom of the *taberna* or tavern, a place in which to meet, drink and do business. A chequerboard was used to indicate a place where games could be played and money exchanged.

The Danes and the Saxons who followed the Romans encouraged the consumption of *öl* or ale. Every home brewed its own ale, using the same cereals as those employed in baking bread. Those who made the best ale, usually women (brewsters), began to offer their product to friends and neighbours. They would signal the arrival of a new brew by placing a pole or ale stake with a garland of evergreens through a window. The ale house, commemorated today as the Bush or Hollybush, had arrived.

The Norman conquerors drank wine (and probably cider) but they took the British habit of beer drinking sufficiently seriously to license manufacturers and to fine those who made bad beer. The spread of Christianity brought many inns under the control of the church. Monks and priests were great brewers – though they preached temperance and moderation to others – and small inns and hostelries developed around every important place of worship for pilgrims to rest and refresh themselves. Ecbright, Archbishop of York in the eighth century, instructed his bishops and priests to provide hospices for pilgrims and travellers. The production in some of the great religious houses was prodigious. Fountains Abbey in Yorkshire had a malthouse that was sixty feet square and its brewhouse produced sixty barrels of strong ale every ten days.

In the Middle Ages considerable efforts were made to control drinking places. They were clearly defined: an ale house only sold drink; a tavern offered food as well; and an inn offered food, drink and accommodation.

A considerable boost was given to drinking in country inns in the thirteenth century when a tax known as a Scot was introduced on ale consumed in licensed premises in towns. Drinkers would thus hurry to village ale houses to drink 'Scot free'. City dwellers today still repair to country pubs in the hope that beer will be cheaper there, but as Robert Louis Stevenson observed, 'It is better to travel hopefully than to arrive'.

By the late Middle Ages the names of inns were firmly established. The earliest had religious associations – the lamb or the mitre – due to their proximity to abbeys and churches. Others took their names from the heraldic devices of the aristocracy, such as red lions or blue boars, while the most obsequious landlords displayed portraits of the king's head or the monarch's coats of arms. In the cities, inns began to take their names from the new associations of traders; country inns followed suit but their names reflected rural occupations such as stonemasonry, quarrying or thatching.

The increasing domination of the towns and cities did not decrease the importance of the country inn. The Turnpike Acts in 1663 allowed good paved roads to be built. Coach travel boomed and new and substantial coaching inns grew up along all the main routes, offering overnight hospitality and stabling as well as food and drink. The inn became a celebrated part of the British way of life as such writers as Samuel Johnson and Charles Dickens travelled the length and breadth of the country and drew inspiration from the many hostelries in which they stayed. 'There is nothing which has yet been contrived by man, by which so much happiness is produced as by a good tavern or inn,' Dr Johnson enthused to James Boswell.

The village pub survives today. The term 'public house' is of Victorian origin and applies more accurately to the new drinking places built by brewers in towns to counteract the misery of the gin palaces. The true inn, tavern and even the occasional ale house, are found mainly in rural areas.

This book has set out to capture an image of the inn at the end of the twentieth century. It is not our aim merely to show the prettiest and most timbered and be-thatched of the breed. That would be a distortion. There are penny plain as well as tuppence coloured in these pages. Together the pubs chosen give a true picture of something that is uniquely English. We have not strayed far beyond the boundaries of England for Scotland and Wales have a quite different pub culture. The three Scottish entries are definably inns but once you move beyond the Borders drinking is done in bars and hotels. And it is worth noting that the most northerly entry in the book is in the English county of Northumberland.

There is much debate about the survival of the English village pub as brewers concentrate on towns and areas where delivery is easy. Rural pubs are vital links in community life, acting as meeting places, village post offices, barbers and polling stations as well as drinking haunts. If pubs close, the communities around them will begin to shrivel and die and Hilaire Belloc's dire warning (quoted on the first page of this book) will have come to pass. This book is both a celebration of the village pub and a small contribution towards its survival.

PREVIOUS PAGE **Tibbie Shiels Inn**, St Mary's Loch, *Borders (see also page 84)*

What is real ale?

All the pubs in this book have one thing in common: they serve what is popularly known as 'real ale' or, in brewers' parlance, cask-conditioned beer. Real ale is the champagne of the beer world. While other types of beer are conditioned in the brewery and often filtered and pasteurized to kill the living yeast, cask beer is encouraged to undergo a secondary fermentation in its container in the pub cellar. Other countries brew living beers, but only Britain produces great quantities of natural beer conditioned in their casks.

Real ale is made from the finest malting barley and choicest English hops and is fermented with quick-acting 'top fermenting' yeast strains. After a short conditioning period in the brewery it is delivered to pubs to complete its maturation in the cask. The methods of brewing and conditioning produce beers of great complexity, with rich fruity and hoppy aromas and flavours. The Campaign for Real Ale has almost single-handedly backed the revival of cask beer and is largely responsible for its current popularity.

Abbey Inn, Byland, *Yorkshire*

The Abbey Inn has arguably the finest setting in the whole of England. It stands across the road from the ruins of Byland Abbey, one of the chain of Cistercian monasteries in the area. The abbey is twelfth-century and was moved, brick by brick and stone by stone, to its present site from Old Byland. Its original setting was deemed to be too close to the great monastery at Rievaulx and led to disputes between the two groups of monks.

West Country

How fine it is to . . . come to some straggling village, with the lights streaming
through the surrounding gloom; and then, after inquiring for the best entertainment
that the place affords, to 'take one's ease at one's inn!'

— WILLIAM HAZLITT, ON GOING ON A JOURNEY

THE FURTHEST TIP OF CORNWALL IS A GREATER DISTANCE FROM LONDON
than the capital is from Scotland but the long and daunting journey by road
does not stop thousands of tourists from descending on the peninsula in the
summer. The reason is not hard to find. Once across the Tamar, you are in a
different country, part of the Celtic fringe. Areas of Cornwall – and its pubs –
may have been ruined by thoughtless modernization and the trinket trade but it
remains a magical land of Celtic crosses, villages named after saints, a temperate
climate and the great beaches sought after by holidaymakers. The climate is so
strikingly different to the rest of the country's that flowers bloom a month earlier
and palm trees grow in the sunniest parts. Inland, the spiny back of Cornwall is
desolate moorland while the long-dead tin mines with their crumbling brick
'castles' topping the now empty shafts mark the once thriving industry.

Truro with its cathedral, Penzance with its fine Regency houses, and Tintagel
with its Arthurian legends are high on every visitor's list, as is Helston, famous
for its floral or furry dance. Helston also has a legendary home-brew pub, the
Blue Anchor, a thatched fifteenth-century ale house with dauntingly strong
Spingo beers. Many of Cornwall's town pubs have been modernized to cater for
the passing trade and you will have to navigate the winding lanes and
idiosyncratic signposting to find the true pub delights. When the county had a
successful industrial base it had a flourishing brewing business, too, but the

breweries have declined in step until just two remain, the Cornish brewery and St Austell.

Devon has fared even worse. Famous breweries in Plymouth and Tiverton have been closed as part of the war of attrition brought to the industry by the giants that now dominate British brewing. There is now no major commercial brewery in the county though a growing number of small, often one-man companies (micros), are providing much-needed choice. As in Cornwall, many of Devon's town pubs have been ruined to please the 'grockles', the mildly defamatory nickname given to summer visitors. (In Cornwall they are called 'emmets', from an Old English word meaning 'ant'.)

Fortunately, the villages retain many delightful and largely unspoilt inns tucked down lanes or providing much needed comfort on the edges of the moors.

Somerset is a Saxon word meaning 'land of the summer people'. The county's tors can be bleak and forbidding, but in general this is gentle, rolling Mendip country with limestone walls, ancient monasteries, and the tiny yet magnificent cathedral city of Wells. Glastonbury Tor, rising starkly from the plains, is topped by the fifteenth-century church of St Michael.

Somerset, too, has suffered from brewery devastation but a handful of sturdy minnows beaver away to produce tasty ales. The West Country is cider country, too. People have been making a drink from the juice of the apple since pre-Roman times, and the Normans introduced the more refined art of cider-making following their invasion. Cider today, even more than beer, is dominated by giant producers, but there are many farms still producing genuine rough and scrumpy varieties of great strength.

PREVIOUS PAGE **Tucker's Grave**, Faulkland, *Somerset* (*see page 154*)
OPPOSITE **Miners Arms**, Mithian, *Cornwall* (*see page 154*)

Peter Tavy Inn
Peter Tavy, *Devon*

Peter Tavy should not be confused with Peter Davey, one of Uncle Tom Cobley's ill-fated revellers. The village and its inn take their name from the church of St Peter that stands on the banks of the River Tavy. The inn is ancient – no one knows quite how old – and is a small moorland pub. The exterior is plain but inviting, with a slate roof and the pub's name on a simple signboard above the door. The beamed bar is superb, with settles set in the deep stone-mullioned windows, larger settles on the black flagstoned floor and a dominating stone fireplace. There is a vast range of beers, most of them tapped straight from the cask.

The pub is part of the 'Dartmoor letter box' scheme: participants have special books stamped in the pub and stamp the pub's own book (shown *right*) in return. There are letter boxes dotted all over the moor, some in secret places, and part of the fun is to find them all. A guide book outlining the scheme is on sale in the county.

St Kew Inn, St Kew, *Cornwall*

The pub cat warms itself in front of the open kitchen range in the bar of the inn: what better indication could there be that this is a truly welcoming *public house*? It is a fifteenth-century stone-built pub in a small village in a wooded hollow: don't confuse St Kew with St Kew Highway a few miles distant. The inn has old meat hooks hanging from the ceiling and the range blasts out marvellous heat when the winter winds whine and roar. The bar serves ale straight from the cask – no new-fangled beer pumps here – and regulars hang their tankards from a beam above the bar. High-backed settles and Windsor chairs are set on the dark Delabole slate floor: Delabole is a Cornish quarry still in use and many local pubs have floors made from its slate.

The inn is haunted by a young girl named Adele: her body was found under the floor some fifteen years ago when repairs were being carried out.

Bush Inn, Morwenstow, *Cornwall*

The Bush (*left*) dates from 950 AD when it was a chapel; a leper's squint hole and a Celtic *piscina* survive from that time. The building has been an ale house since 1250 and is reputed to be haunted. The propeller from the De Havilland Gipsy Moth that Amy Johnson flew to Australia in 1930 decorates one wall. There are spectacular cliff walks nearby, and Hawker's Hut, a four-seater shack that is owned by the National Trust.

Crown Inn, St Ewe, *Cornwall*

The whitewashed old cottage inn dates from the sixteenth century and has been run by the same Cornish family for more than thirty years. Inside there are atmospheric low beams, flagstoned floors, a four-hundred-year-old high-backed settle and a fireplace with an ancient roasting spit; the centrepiece of the inn is a collection of fine pewter. The village gets its unusual name from a local saint.

Drewe Arms, Drewsteignton, *Devon*

This is Mabel Mudge's pub. No one locally speaks of the Drewe Arms: they go to 'Aunty Mabel's' for a drink. This simple old thatched ale house was built to accommodate the construction workers on the village church. Mabel is in her nineties, claims to be England's oldest licensee – and who would gainsay her – and has lived in the pub since 1919. She holds court in the bar, recalls the days of horse-drawn traffic in the village and, when her arthritis is bad, invites you to draw your own glass of ale or cider from the casks stillaged behind the servery.

The name of the pub was originally the Druid's Arms but was changed in honour of Julius Drewe. He was founder of the Home and Colonial Stores chain for whom Sir Edwin Lutyens built between 1910 and 1930 the nearby and sinisterly-named Castle Drogo above the Teign gorge, the last castle to be built in England and open to the public.

Star Inn, St Just-in-Penwith, *Cornwall*

Locals call the Star 'the last *proper* pub in Cornwall'. Close to Land's End and Cape Cornwall it defies the ravages of tourism by remaining a simple old inn in a village that was once at the heart of the tin-mining industry. It is built of rugged stone, mellowed at the back by climbing plants. A mounting block by the entrance stresses that the Star was a coaching inn on a main route through the peninsula in the days before steam and motor cars. The L-shaped bar has many seagoing and mining artefacts, including miners' lamps and, as befits St Just's oldest inn, is often packed with locals. A small room called the Snuggery is used by families and the old game of table skittles (shown *right*) can be played.

Masons Arms, Knowstone, *Devon*

The Masons Arms is a thirteenth-century
unspoilt farm pub opposite the village church in a
remote part of Exmoor. The exterior is thatched
and whitewashed while the small main bar has
head-cracking low beams, a stone floor, and a
fireplace with a bread oven and rustic furniture.
A collection of ancient and modern bottles hang
from the beams and the walls are decorated with
farming tools.

Normandy Arms, Blackawton, *Devon*

The fifteenth-century origins of the Normandy
Arms are inscribed on the whitewashed exterior
but in truth this is a much-modernized pub and
none the worse for it. The Normandy theme is
played up with photos of Field Marshal
Montgomery and the D-Day landings; the
surrounding area, the South Hams, was
extensively used in preparation for the Second
World War assault on the French coast.

Tom Cobley Tavern
Spreyton, *Devon*

The tavern has been licensed since 1589 and will have had a different name then as Tom Cobley (or Cobleigh) and his friends didn't set off for Widecombe Fair (or Widdicombe: spelling is splendidly leave-it-to-you in these parts) on Tom Pearse's grey mare until 1802. The pub, with its striking thatched porched entrance and tubs of flowers and hanging baskets, has a fine portrait (shown *right*) of the village's famous son hanging above the open fireplace. The fame of Tom Cobley attracts visitors like a magnet and the pub can be crowded in summer. If the landlord asks you where you come from, don't be put off: it's just that he serves people from the 'wrong' part of Devon last.

Masons Arms, Branscombe, *Devon*

There is a feeling of peace and great age in the Masons Arms, a fourteenth-century inn built of mellow creeper-covered stone in a village of lovely thatched cottages. The main bar of the inn is outstanding, dominated by a large fireplace with a log fire which is still used to spit-roast joints. The bar has a low beamed ceiling, rough whitewashed walls, a grandfather clock and settles on the flagstoned floor. Darts, dominoes and shove ha'penny are played in the inn. Surrounded by wooded hills, Branscombe is a fine base for exploring the Devon-Dorset coastal region: the sea is close by, Lyme Regis is just over the border and the Donkey Sanctuary nearby.

The George Inn
Norton St Philip, *Somerset*

The George has been an inn for six hundred years and was built to accommodate merchants trading in wool and cloth with nearby Hinton Priory. The street side of the pub has a massive oak door under a great stone porch, mullioned windows, exposed beams on the first and second floors and an intriguing flight of steps leading up to a small landing and door used for loading. The style of the back of the pub (shown *left*) is in stark contrast to the front.

The main bar has beams hung with horse tackle, high windows, settles and simple wooden seats, plain tables and bare floorboards. A panelled lounge has more antique settles while off the courtyard is the Dungeon Bar, a reminder that supporters of the Duke of Monmouth were imprisoned here after the failure of his ludicrously ill-prepared 'pitchfork rebellion' in the seventeenth century. Behind the pub you can stroll across the meadows to the medieval church whose bells, according to Samuel Pepys in 1668, are 'mighty tuneable'.

Black Horse, Clapton in Gordano, *Avon*

The whitewashed fourteenth-century pub is tucked away down a remote country lane in the Gordano valley but at night you can see the glow of Bristol a few miles away. The pub's main bar has a part-flagstoned and part-tiled floor with winged settles and built-in wall benches, photos and cartoons of the pub, and a welcoming log fire in a large inglenook with horse stirrups and old flintlock guns on the mantelbeam. A window in the snug remains barred, recalling the days in the nineteenth century when the room was a local magistrate's jail. Today mugs hang from the beams and the room contains some superb settles, one donated by the Motor Racing Club of North Somerset, another with an Art Nouveau insert with the curiously Scottish sentiment 'East, West, Hame's Best'. A third room can be used by families and has traditional pub games. Landlord Tom Shaw is only the fourth licensee of the pub this century.

Rising Sun
Gunnislake, *Cornwall*

The simple whitewashed exterior of this seventeenth-century pub in the Tamar Valley scarcely prepares you for the explosion of riotous colour inside. The pub has three rooms and a family area. Mrs Hughes, the landlady, has decorated the pub with jugs, plates, potties and a large collection of photos and souvenirs of the Royal Family, dating back to Queen Victoria's time. Beer lovers will find a wide range of ales, including such West Country specialities as St Austell's Hicks Special. Gunnislake was once a mining area and stands proud on a steep hill above the Tamar.

Royal Oak
Luxborough, *Somerset*

The whitewashed, L-shaped inn stands on an old coaching route in a tuck in the Brendon Hills. It has been a pub since the seventeenth century but is considerably older than that: it is believed to have been an inn with the intriguing name of the Blazing Stump as early as the fifteenth century. Landlord Robin Stamp declares: 'When you walk through the door you will think you have stepped back two centuries and you won't have changed your mind when you leave'. Its three fine rooms have a wealth of beams, flagstoned and cobbled floors, inglenooks, simple furnishings and log fires. Locals play dominoes, cribbage and darts with great enthusiasm, and there is a good selection of West Country beers.

Rock Inn, Haytor Vale, *Devon*

Haytor Vale nestles in the lee of Hay Tor, the bleak and biggest outcrop on Dartmoor, and the Rock makes a fine resting place for walkers. Dartmoor National Park (within which the pub lies) offers horse riding, golf, fishing and walking. The whitewashed exterior and dormers in the slate roof beckon across the countryside.

The inn has been sensitively modernized to offer most creature comforts but its history has not been buried. Down the centuries it has been an ale house for granite quarrymen on the moors and iron miners, a meeting place for farmers and landowners, and a coaching inn. It is a warren of rooms with half-panelled walls, Windsor chairs, settles, log fires and a plethora of old prints of the area.

Wessex

It was of the most beautiful colour that the eye of an artist in beer could ever desire;
full in body, yet brisk as a volcano; piquant, yet without a twang; luminous as an
autumn sunset; free from streakiness of taste but finally, rather heady.
— THOMAS HARDY, THE TRUMPET MAJOR, *on the beer of 'Casterbridge'*
(Dorchester)

WESSEX WAS ONCE AN ANCIENT KINGDOM BUT IT IS NOW AN UNOFFICIAL tourist region indelibly stamped with the name of Hardy. Dorchester has a statue of the great novelist and poet while the town's museum houses a room modelled on his study. His cottage is preserved by the National Trust at Higher Bockhampton. Dorset has its fair share of summer visitors but many only pause as they rush headlong for the West Country, so the towns and villages have suffered fewer ravages at their hands. The Isle of Purbeck is the most remote area, dominated by the awesome ruins of Corfe Castle, the unspoilt old seaside town of Swanage and the sweeping beaches around Studland. Lyme Regis is a delightful little harbour town made famous in John Fowles's *The French Lieutenant's Woman.*

Inland there are countless unspoilt old villages, with unusual names such as Lytchett Minster, Tarrant Monkton and Worth Matravers that derive from feudal landowning families. Several villages contain the curious word Piddle or Puddle in their name. This stems from the legend that the Devil once piddled all over the area to create its rivers and streams. Tolpuddle, a cheery village today, has a grim place in the history books: it was here that the first agricultural trade union was formed. Its founders were sentenced in Dorchester and sent as criminals to Australia.

Wiltshire is a county with more than its fair share of prehistoric sites, of which Stonehenge is the most famous, with others at Avebury, Silbury Hill and West Kennet Long Barrow. There are the remains of Iron Age hill forts while Old Sarum, the original site of Salisbury before the cathedral was built and most famous of the 'rotten boroughs', can still be seen. Wiltshire is downs land, grazed by contented sheep. The Kennet and Avon canal manages to stagger into Devizes up a ladder of twenty-nine locks. The old market town's name comes from *les divises*, Old French for boundaries: a Norman bishop built a castle here on the boundary between his land and that of the king. Thriving towns and villages include Marlborough, with its one long, winding street, Bradford-on-Avon, once a centre of the cloth trade, and Lacock, a medieval village preserved by the National Trust, with the Fox Talbot Museum of Photography.

Hampshire is a patchwork county of rolling downs and wooded tracks but its coastline is dominated by the great bustling industrial centres of Gosport, Portsmouth and Southampton. Inland, Winchester was once the capital of England and has a wealth of fine buildings. Among the many fine smaller towns, Alresford is famous for its steam railway, which has the charming name of the Watercress Line.

Hampshire has a renowned traditional brewer in Gale's of Horndean while the Ringwood Brewery was at the centre of the new small brewery revolution. Wiltshire has a good clutch of brewers, include Wadworth's of 6X fame in Devizes, and two in the old railway town of Swindon. Dorset is well-studded with breweries, too: Eldridge Pope are a major force in Dorchester and produce a Thomas Hardy's Ale with which to toast the scribe, Hall and Woodhouse have a handsome brewery in the equally handsome Georgian town of Blandford Forum, while Palmer's of Bridport is the only brewery to have a partly-thatched brewhouse.

PREVIOUS PAGE **Compasses**, Chicksgrove, *Wiltshire (see page 154)*
OPPOSITE **Hurdlers Arms**, Binley, *Hampshire (see page 154)*

Boot, Littledown, *Hampshire*

The flint-faced Boot was built in the fifteenth century and looks it, with small windows peeping out like startled eyes from under the curved thatched roof and a porched door like a questing nose. It was originally a cobblers, hence the name, and there is a collection of miniature old boots and shoes in two cabinets in the pub and other more modern footware hangs from the ceiling. The two pub signs – left and right leather riding boot – belonged to a former landlord.

Inside all is tranquillity in the two connecting bars with low beams and white-panelled walls; one bar has an inglenook with a log fire, the other has a darts board. A good range of ales comes straight from casks set up on trestles. A conservatory extension is used by diners and you can play traditional pub games. The black plague in the seventeenth century destroyed nearby Vernham Dean but Littledown and its magical inn survived.

Jolly Sailor
Bursledon, *Hampshire*

The name of this riverside pub is built into the frontage and shouts at you from the jetty. This is yachting country and the pub overlooks the River Hamble and is part of a busy marina. The Jolly Sailor featured in a successful TV series called 'Howard's Way'. The brick-built building, with imposing dormers, bow windows and two old ship's figure-heads above the entrance, has been a pub for just over 60 years; surprisingly, before that it was a vicarage. The back bar has a delightful air with its beamed ceiling, flagstoned floor, settles and old church pews around an open fire while the oak-floored front bar is furnished with Windsor chairs and settles. Pictures of ships line the walls and shells in a net hang from the ceiling. Close by is the thirteenth-century church built by the Benedictine monks of Hamble le Rys.

Square & Compass, Worth Matravers, *Dorset*

Ray Newman, like a Biblical prophet in a Cecil B. De Mille movie, presides with flowing grey locks and beard over this splendid old ale house that has been in his family for more than eighty-five years. The Square & Compass, which takes its name from the tools of local quarrymen, was first licensed 265 years ago. It was formerly a farm and its history stretches back to the time of the Normans' Domesday Book.

Chickens scratch in the yard in front of the pub where you can sit in the sun on benches and look across the fields to St Alban's Head and the grey-green sea beyond. Inside, a narrow corridor takes you to a hatch where the Newman family draw beer straight from casks stillaged in a cool side room. Customers can drink in the corridor, which houses a collection of fossils, or in the sunny parlour with old tables, wall seats and local pictures and cartoons.

Royal Oak, Cerne Abbas, *Dorset*

This showplace Dorset village with houses of orange stone and flint is famous for its ruined abbey and the rude and rampant figure of the Romano-British Cerne Giant cut into the chalk hills above. The village once sported no fewer than thirteen inns and ale houses as a result of the steady flood of pilgrims to the abbey. The number is now down to three. The Royal Oak is a Tudor inn built of sturdy stone and smothered in creeper. Inside there is a polished ramble of connected rooms, alcoves, nooks and crannies with some wood-panelled walls, log fires, horse brasses and plates and cups hanging from the beams.

Wye Valley and Malverns

Oh I have been to Ludlow fair
And left my necktie God knows where,
And carried half way home, or near,
Pints and quarts of Ludlow beer:
Then the world seemed none so bad,
And I myself a sterling lad;
And down in lovely muck I've lain,
Happy till I woke again.

— A. E. HOUSMAN

THIS IS SUCH HAUNTINGLY LOVELY COUNTRY, LARGELY UNMOLESTED BY the industrial revolution, that it is hard to believe that the land was once as bitterly contested as the other border region between England and Scotland. Yet Offa's Dyke runs the entire length of the Welsh border and much blood was spilt over the centuries in the battles for Welsh independence and to win back land that belonged to them. To judge by the numbers of Evans's, Jones's and Roberts's who live on the English side of the border, quite a few Welshmen and women have slipped through the net.

The area is dominated by the great river of the Wye, seen at its finest from the outcrop of Symonds Yat or from the little market town of Ross-on-Wye. As industrialization largely bypassed it, village after village and town after town recall less frenetic times with their panoply of half-timbered and rough plastered buildings. Weobley is perhaps the finest preserved town, a breath-catching vista of black-and-white houses. There is a marble monument to a Colonel Birch, a parliamentarian who captured the town for Cromwell, changed sides and helped put a Stuart back on the throne. Leominster (pronounced 'Lemster') was for five hundred years one of the great wool markets of England. Malvern has strong links with Edward Elgar and the designated Malvern Trail will take you to all the places of interest in this gentle area, including the British Camp hill fort. This is cider country just as much as the better-known West Country. Hereford is home to the world's biggest cider maker, Bulmer's, and there are many smaller makers up country lanes and on farms. Some of them still make tiny amounts of perry from special varieties of pears, once a major industry in the region.

Gloucestershire is dominated by the gentle sweep and curve of the majestic Severn. Its villages are tranquil and Gloucester can lay claim to arguably the finest of the region's many great cathedrals.

To the north Shropshire was as fiercely fought over by English and Welsh and later Roundheads and Cavaliers as the softer country below. We are getting closer to the industrial heartland of England but Shropshire – ancient Salopia – remains a rural land of hills and valleys with views of ten counties from the eery Stiperstones. Ludlow has a medieval bridge, a castle, a cobbled Broad Street and the much-photographed Feathers Hotel, all timbers and moulding, seemingly kept upright only by the buildings on either side. Stokesay Castle is a fine example of a fortified manor house while Bishop's Castle has one of the best-known home-brew pubs, the Three Tuns. Across the border into Cheshire the towns and villages roll on in splendour with more half-timbered delights, personified by the county town itself.

Warrington has declined as a major brewing town but has one giant and one minnow. Hereford and Worcester has two micros, a number shared by Shropshire. Gloucestershire has the vigorous Uley micro and Donnington in its magical setting at Stow-on-the-Wold.

PREVIOUS PAGE **Donnington Brewery,** near Stow-on-the-Wold, *Gloucestershire*
OPPOSITE **Boat Inn**, Ashleworth Quay, *Gloucestershire (see page 154)*

Rhydspence Inn
Whitney-on-Wye, *Hereford & Worcester*

The inn is on the border of England and Wales – in fact it *is* the border, marked by a stream running through the garden. The commanding black-and-white half-timbered building lies back from the Hereford to Brecon road, standing sentinel-like over the border crossing and the great sweep of the Wye Valley beyond. The Rhydspence Inn – pronounced 'Ridspence' – was built in the sixteenth century as a resting place for Welsh drovers taking their sheep to market. The carefully restored inn has two small connected beamed bars warmed by a log fire, where locals play cribbage, dominoes and quoits. Creature comforts are provided by old chairs and cushioned wall benches built into the timbered walls.

Old Bull
Inkberrow, *Hereford &*
Worcester

The bulging half-timbered walls of
the sixteenth-century inn seem to
defy gravity but it has been standing
for so long that it will survive
another century or two. It is in the
centre of a cheerful village of stone
and half-timbered houses on the
Stratford and Worcester road. The
lounge has oak beams and trusses
and high-backed settles, set off by a
vast inglenook fireplace. The inn is
the model for the Bull in the radio
soap opera, The Archers. There are
signed photographs of the stars of
the show and press cuttings about it,
too. Claims that William
Shakespeare slept in the inn and that
Charles II sought refuge there after
the battle of Worcester in 1651 are
probably as fictional as The Archers.
In summer you can enjoy the view of
the inn, with its steeply-pitched red
tiled roof and dormers, from
benches and tables on the forecourt.

Plough
Wistanstow, *Shropshire*

The border country is unusually rich in pubs that brew their own beer and the Plough is owned by the thrusting and successful Wood Brewery, which is housed in a separate and older building alongside the pub. Its brews include one called simply Wonderful – no false modesty here – and a strong winter ale called Christmas Cracker. The brews are, naturally, on sale in the Plough which has a striking high-raftered lounge with a large bottle collection. Farm ciders and bottled beers complement the house ales. Wistanstow is in fine walking country, close to the Welsh border, Bishop's Castle with its home-brew pub, the Three Tuns, and Ludlow with its castle and stunning architecture.

Sun Inn, Clun, *Shropshire*

'The quietest place under the sun', said
A. E. Housman of Clun, which belies the
bloody history of this border area near Offa's
Dyke, built to keep the Welsh at bay. Offa wasn't
entirely successful, and so Clun Castle was added
in the eleventh century. The inn is relatively
modern, built in the fifteenth century of cruck
design in which great curved timbers support the
roof. Inside, the bar has a wealth of exposed
beams, flagstones, settles and a huge fireplace
decorated with ancient crooks and fire irons.
Beer is served by a Victorian 'cash register' beer
engine. There are more beams and settles in the
lounge. A sheltered back terrace is made
colourful by geraniums and other pot plants. In
Clun you can visit the castle and museum and
cross the river by an old saddleback bridge.

Heart of England

Blessings of your heart, you brew good ale.
WILLIAM SHAKESPEARE, TWO GENTLEMEN OF VERONA, *inscribed above*
The Vine pub, known as the Bull and Bladder, in Brierley Hill, West Midlands,
brewery tap for Batham's brewery.

THIS IS BOTH SHAKESPEARE COUNTRY AND THE BLACK COUNTRY, THE former an idyllic pastoral land of thatched and timber-framed buildings, the latter the centre of the industrial revolution that created dynamic new technologies but caused terrible havoc to the environment with belching chimneys and fouled-up rivers. The region also houses a small and otherwise nondescript town that was the centre of a brewing revolution that followed other changes in industry. Monks had brewed in and around Burton-on-Trent as early as the eleventh century and had found the spring waters of the area ideal for producing ales of great quality. But it was in the late eighteenth century that Burton began to rival London as a great brewing centre. London, with its soft waters, brewed dark porter and stout beers. But the soil of Burton was rich in calcium sulphate – gypsum – and the spring waters bubbling to the surface produced light and sparkling ales with the aid of such new technologies as refrigeration, yeast cultivation and improved curing of malt and hops.

Light and quenching beers were brewed first for the thirsty troops and civil servants in India but these 'India Pale Ales' achieved great popularity at home thanks to the arrival of the steam train and they soon supplanted London's darker beers in popularity. London brewers rushed to Burton to open new plants there and the small Staffordshire town became the capital of the brewing industry and

made great fortunes for the likes of William Bass and William Worthington. Bass has a fascinating brewery museum in the town while Marston's brewery still uses the 'union room' system of brewing in which beers ferment inside great oak casks: both museum and brewery are open for inspection.

To the north of the region is Derbyshire's gritstone Peak District, beloved by both climbers and pot-holers. The area has been the scene of many pitched battles between ramblers and landowners; the confrontation at Kinder Scout has gone down in walkers' history – they won there the right to go where they choose. Edale marks the start of the Pennine Way and both landscape and dialect are beginning to shade into the gritty north. In Derbyshire you can enjoy the market town of Bakewell and its famous tarts, the Jacobean castle at Bolsover, the 'palace of the peak' at Chatsworth built by the Dukes of Devonshire and you can venture underground in the caverns at Castleton, where the waters, incidentally, were once much praised by local brewers.

Nottinghamshire was once a major coal-mining area, and D. H. Lawrence's home in Eastwood is open to visitors. Nottingham has a famous castle and the oldest inn in England, The Trip to Jerusalem. Leicestershire is a county of spires and squires and retains a strong hunting tradition to the distress of many. The creation of Rutland Water, a huge reservoir, is a popular attraction for water sports enthusiasts.

Northamptonshire, to the east, is almost a forgotten county and has retained many splendid villages and a wealth of fine stone buildings. Its main deficiency is a single functioning brewery, a fate shared by Warwickshire. Leicestershire has four independents and Nottinghamshire two. Derbyshire has just one small micro but Staffordshire maintains a good tradition with five breweries in Burton and another in Burslem while the West Midlands, as befits the heart of the industrial region, has ten beer producers.

PREVIOUS PAGE **Royal Oak,** Whatcote, *Warwickshire* (*see page 154*)
OPPOSITE **Red House**, Knipton, *Leicestershire* (*see page 154*)

Crown, Old Dalby, *Leicestershire*

The Crown is some way off the Melton Mowbray thoroughfare, reached by a gated road. The inn is most un-publike, a huddle of red-brick buildings at different levels. It looks more like a farmhouse, which is how it began in 1690. It stands in a narrow lane, and you enter round the back where, surprisingly, there are impressively sweeping lawns. Just as impressive as you enter is the enormous range of ales tapped straight from casks in a servery: there are beers from all over the country but you can count on some Midlands specialities such as Hardy & Hansons ales from Kimberley. There are several tiny rooms, with beams, ancient oak settles, Windsor chairs and open fires. The pub is always ablaze with fresh flowers and there are hunting prints on the walls. It is very much a sporting pub and the national pétanque championship is staged here; the local fox hunt, the Quorn, also meets at the Crown.

Case is Altered
Five Ways, Haseley Knob, *Warwickshire*

A whitewashed cottage pub with both a fascinating name and history stands in a narrow lane and resists such twentieth-century intrusions as music or fruit machines. Even the bar billiards table has to be fed pre-decimal sixpences. You reach the entrance through a wrought-iron gate and a small paved courtyard. The main bar has a few leather-covered settles on a tiled floor and some tables. An old poster depicts the long defunct Lucas, Blackwell & Arkwright brewery while a clock spells out the name of Hornleys, another deceased producer of beer. The lounge (*right*), with carved oak furniture and copper jugs, is used at weekends and is presided over by the matriarchal landlady Mary Gwendoline Jones.

The pub is a modern mix of a former cottage, ale house and bakers and was run by another matriarch in the nineteenth century called Mercedes Griffiths. When she finally won a legal battle to sell spirits as well as beer the pub changed its name to its present one because the licence had been changed by the magistrates – the case was altered.

Olde Gate Inn
Brassington, *Derbyshire*

The snug is the high spot of this creeper-clad pub, with its seventeenth-century kitchen range, scrubbed tables, gleaming copper pots, pewter mugs hanging from a beam, an ancient clock and stone mullioned windows with a view across the garden to the surrounding pasture land. Though the pub bears the date 1874 it was originally built in 1616 of limestone and timbers salvaged from the wrecks of the Spanish Armada, which were exchanged for valuable lead mined in the area. A second beamed bar to the left of a lobby with a serving hatch has some old panelled settles and a fire under a mantelbeam. Darts, dominoes and cribbage are played and there are a few benches at the front of the pub where you can hear the villagers practising bell-ringing in the church on Friday evenings.

Martins Arms
Colston Bassett
Nottinghamshire

A splendidly rustic pub in an idyllic village setting, it takes its name from the farming family that turned it into an ale house in 1690. The whitewashed pub has an imposing porched entrance and, inside, the massive Tudor fireplace and matching bar came from the library in Colston Bassett Hall. The garden includes a bowling green, which was installed for local teams but visitors are welcome to use it. Colston Bassett is in the Vale of Belvoir and has strong hunting connections.

Old Coach House
Ashby St Ledgers
Northamptonshire

The Gunpowder Plot was hatched in this stone-built former farmhouse and at nearby Althorp Hall in a village of stone and thatched houses and wide verges. The pub was hideously modernized in the 1960s, and the present owners deserve great praise for their devotion to unearthing a wealth of old inglenooks and stone floors. The lounge bar has impressive high-backed and winged settles on red and black tiles, standing timbers decorated with horse brasses, and a log fire. Table skittles, darts and dominoes are played in the front bar. Should you arrive by horse they will be happy to look after it in the stables.

The Star
West Leake, *Nottinghamshire*

The Star is known to locals as the Pit House: nothing to do with coal mines for the old coaching inn once staged cockfights. Close to the Derbyshire border, the pub stands well back from its country lane and is identified by a free-standing inn sign. The rough, whitewashed walls are relieved by flowering window boxes and tubs, with seats on the forecourt. To the left as you enter there is a friendly public bar with settles round oak tables, a tiled floor, harness, whips, foxes' masks and, inevitably, cockfighting prints on the ochre-painted walls. The lounge to the right is half-panelled and has a welcoming log fire and comfortable armchairs.

The Lakes
and Scottish Borders

O, Mortal man, that lives by bread,
What is it makes thy nose so red?
Thou silly fool, that looks so pale,
'Tis drinking Sally Birkett's Ale
— sign of the MORTAL MAN *pub at* TROUTBECK

THE LAKE DISTRICT, FOR ALL ITS FAME, IS A TINY AREA, BUT THAT IS ITS charm. The mountains and lakes seem tall and deep only in comparison to the minuscule size of the region, and the compression means that packed within it are places of beauty at every turn. In Scotland you have to drive for hours from loch to loch but here there is a lake round every corner. The snow-capped peaks, the mysterious watery depths and the dark screes of rock that fall sheer-sided into them, and the wooded slopes tinted with gold in autumn attract visitors by the car-load and have been a source of inspiration to writers and poets. Both of Wordsworth's homes, Dove Cottage at Grasmere and Rydal Mount, are open to the public. Beatrix Potter's humble home at Hill Top Farm, Near Sawrey, is also open to visitors. There are ferries on Windermere and the 'Laal Ratty' Ravenglass to Eskdale steam railway runs through seven miles of enchanted countryside in the Esk valley.

Cartmel is a village dominated by a priory church. Penrith is a good base for two of the loveliest lakes, Ulverston and Derwent Water. Penrith means 'red town' and it was originally built of red sandstone. It has the ruins of a castle hastily built in an effort to keep out the marauding Scots. Hadrian's Wall, which marked the boundary of the Roman push north, lies close to the town. Cockermouth to the west was the birthplace of Fletcher Christian who led the mutiny on the Bounty and today is home for Jenning's brewery, producers of wonderfully tart and fruity beers.

To the east Northumbria is wonderfully open and magnificent countryside, so peacefully free from hordes of tourists that it is hard to believe that this border area was for centuries the scene of bloody skirmishes between Scots and English. Berwick-on-Tweed has officially been in both countries; the present sensible compromise is that it is in England but its football team plays in the Scottish league. There is certainly no finer way to enter Scotland than to be carried over the Tweed on the railway viaduct.

The Scottish borders is a region of wooded valleys and fast-running streams, dotted with small craggy towns and villages. It has strong connections with Sir Walter Scott and John Buchan; there is a small brewery at Buchan's birthplace at Broughton. Traquair House at Innerleithen is Scotland's oldest inhabited stately house and has a restored medieval brewhouse.

The coast south of Berwick is a magical place with the great bulk of Bamburgh Castle, the lovely little harbour of Alnmouth, Craster where they smoke their famous kippers and the lonely beauty of Lindisfarne or Holy Island, reached by causeway at low tide. Inland, Alnwick (pronounced 'Annick') is a sturdily walled old town while, further south, Hexham is a thirteenth-century market town with an abbey dating back much earlier to 664 AD. The village of Cambo has some fine cottage gardens as befits the birthplace of Capability Brown. Blanchland, named after the White Canon monks, has a castellated gatehouse and rows of cottages around a central gravelled square. Northumberland and Durham have just one small micro brewery apiece. Cumbria is better placed with three micros and a home-brew pub to add to the joys of Jennings.

PREVIOUS PAGE **Rose and Crown**, Romaldkirk, *Yorkshire (see page 154)*
OPPOSITE **Tower Bank Arms**, Near Sawrey, *Cumbria (see page 154)*

Sun Inn, Dent, *Cumbria*

There are Yorkshiremen who say that Dent is in 'God's Own Country'. It is not true – though it is close to the county boundary – but you can understand why they wish to lay claim to this old rough stone and whitewashed pub with its own tiny brewery in a converted barn. The bar of the Sun has beams studded with coins, a coal fire, old Schweppes advertisements and local photos.

Crook Inn, Tweedsmuir, *Borders*

There has been an inn on the site since the fourteenth century. The present one dates from 1590 and it is thought to be Scotland's oldest licensed premises. It was a clandestine meeting place for the outlawed seventeenth-century Covenanters and takes its name from a landlady named Jeannie o' the Crook who hid a fugitive from the dragoons in a peat stack. The stone fireplace was built around a cartwheel which was set alight to leave a circular hearth.

Hole in't Wall
Bowness-on-Windermere
Cumbria

The correct but scarcely used name for this back-street pub is the New Hall Inn but it is known to all and sundry by its *nom de bière*. The inn was once smaller and next door was a blacksmith's. The smithy needed copious amounts of ale because of the heat of his work. To avoid going round to the pub he agreed with the landlord that they would knock a hole in the wall between the two buildings so that pots of beer could be passed through to him. The smithy has gone and the pub has expanded to take up his space.

It has a vast fireplace stacked either side with logs, wall seats, beamed ceilings and slate floors. The upper bar is panelled with a fine plaster ceiling and there are rustic farm tools on the walls. The bar has a collection of banknotes behind it while one ceiling is decked out with a collection of chamber pots. There is seating on a patio in warm weather, but don't forget to see the blacksmith's hole. Bowness, a charming small town with some good restaurants, lies by the shore of England's largest lake.

Riverside Inn, Canonbie, *Dumfries*

The gentle ticking of a long-case clock is the only
intrusive sound in this splendid old inn by the
River Esk. The solidly-built stone building is an
elegant hostelry with a peaceful garden; the
connecting bar and lounge have oak beams and
open fires, comfortable chairs, stuffed wildlife
and pictures of the area. The inn has a particularly
fine example of a free-standing sign showing a
dipper on the river shore.

Tibbie Shiels Inn, St Mary's Loch, *Borders*

The ancient inn is named after Isabella Shiels, a
widow with six children who lived in the
eighteenth century; her husband was a mole
catcher who had worked for the local landlord,
Lord Napier; he established her in the little
cottage by the loch to run a hostelry for
travellers. The pub was visited by Sir Walter
Scott and James Hogg, the shepherd poet of
Ettrick, who befriended her.

Masons Arms
Strawberry Bank, Cartmel
Fell, *Cumbria*

The remote old inn was once a secret meeting place of the Kendal Freemasons but you don't need to roll your trouser leg to get in today. Licensee Nigel Stevenson brews his own beer in his mini-brew house on the premises: Amazon, Big Six, Captain Flint and Great Northern ales are dedicated to children's writer Arthur Ransome of *Swallows and Amazons* fame. You can enjoy these or an enormous range of international beers in cheerful rooms with beamed ceilings and flagstoned floors and a log fire. A small lounge has some fine Jacobean panelling, a third room behind the serving counter has a fire in an attractive open range (shown here), and there is a separate room for families. A terrace with rustic seats is a fine vantage spot for the views over the Winster Valley to Whitbarrow Scar.

Black Bull
Etal, *Northumberland*

It's a long journey to this remote hamlet hard-by the Scottish border but you suddenly find yourself in a setting that seems to have been carefully and lovingly preserved from the early part of the twentieth century. The Black Bull is considerably older, stretching back three hundred years. It has a thatched roof at two levels, rough cast white-painted walls and a free standing inn sign in front of lawns and flower beds. The interior was once – in the manner of old rural pubs – several small rooms but they have been knocked through into one, yet still retain a lot of character and there are stone fireplaces at both ends. In the village you can see the ruins of a castle on the River Till and visit the working watermill at Heatherslaw and the restored Ford Castle not far away.

Yorkshire

It was on the great northern road from York to London, about the beginning of October, and about the hour of eight in the evening, that four travellers were, by a violent shower of rain, driven for shelter into a little public-house on the side of the highway, distinguished by a sign which was said to exhibit the figure of a black lion. The kitchen, in which they were assembled, was the only room for entertainment in the house, paved with red bricks, remarkably clean, furnished with three or four Windsor chairs, adorned with shining plates of pewter, and copper saucepans nicely scoured, that even dazzled the eyes of the beholder; while a cheerful fire of seacoal blazed in the chimney.

— TOBIAS SMOLLETT, SIR LANCELOT GREAVES

THIS, TO A PROUD YORKSHIREMAN OR WOMAN, IS 'GOD'S OWN COUNTRY'. In or out of their cups, they will speak of the unrivalled beauty of the moors and the dales and will bemoan the loss of parts of the former ridings to such modern monstrosities as Cleveland and Humberside. They will also claim that their beer is the best (arguable) and the strongest (untrue, but they will not accept views to the contrary).

They certainly demand and enjoy a bigger head of froth on their beer than in other parts of Britain, a result of the method of fermentation developed in Yorkshire. The 'Yorkshire square' is a stone-built, two-storeyed vessel: the fermenting beer gushes up from the bottom level into the top through a central hole, leaving a slurry of yeast behind. The vigour of the fermentation and the reaction with the walls of the vessel create a high and natural level of carbonation which helps create the foaming head on

the beer in the pub. The system is alive and well in Sam Smith's strictly traditional brewery in Tadcaster where horse-drawn drays deliver the beer in wooden casks to the surrounding pubs. Tadcaster, known as the 'Burton of the North', has a small Bass brewery as well as John Smith's with its striking tall, hooped chimney. The Smiths are related and a row at the turn of the century sent one branch up the road to set up a rival establishment.

The tangy beers of the region can be enjoyed in old village pubs deep in the dales or high on the moors to the north. In the dales, as in Derbyshire, there are caverns and pot-holes to visit, old mills to see, the Yorkshire Dales Railway and the Pennine canal to travel on. Skipton is a thriving market town with famous pork pies.

To the north the roads climb ever higher on to the moors, sometimes bleak and desolate but warm and welcoming in the sun. Not to be outdone by the Dales, there is a North Yorks Moors Railway that potters around recalling the great age of steam. Rievaulx – rye valley – is the grandest of the chain of Cistercian abbeys in the area: the abbot chose the site for both its solitude and the quality of the water, an important consideration when monks brewed their own ale. To the east the moors go tumbling into the sea; the coastal area has such charming villages and towns as Robin Hood's Bay, which has no known links with the man of Sherwood, and Whitby with its incongruous Dracula connection.

This is good ale drinking territory. As well as the Smiths of Tadcaster there is the equally famous Theakston's of Masham, brewing their Old Peculier ale in a stone-built brewery that still employs a cooper, and there are some seven other smaller breweries in North Yorkshire. West Yorkshire is well endowed and includes the superb Timothy Taylor beers from Keighley. Only South Yorkshire is poorly provided.

PREVIOUS PAGE **Clive Hollis**, the cooper at Theakston's Brewery, Masham, *North Yorkshire*
OPPOSITE **Hare Inn**, Scawton, *Yorkshire* (*see page 154*)

Falcon, Arncliffe, *Yorkshire*

A dish to set before a queen: beneath the impressive royal insignia above the hatch, David Miller, brother of licensee Rob Miller, pours ale served from casks behind the bar. A modern handpump would seem slightly surprising in this superb old Dales pub with its bay windows and ivy-covered exterior. It has been in the hands of the Miller family for four generations and there are numerous watercolours decorating the place which were painted by David's and Robin's father, who exhibited at the Royal Academy in London.

The Falcon is popular with fell walkers who have tackled or plan to tackle the walk to Malham Tarn, reached by a bridleway. The hatch serves two small rooms with settles, cast-iron tables and fires while a conservatory at the back is used by families. The pub has fishing rights on the local River Skirfare. Charles Kingsley stayed in Arncliffe while he was writing *The Water Babies*.

Laurel Inn, Robin Hood's Bay, *Yorkshire*

The tall and narrow Laurel is on a bend halfway down the cliff and is one of the smallest pubs in Yorkshire. The beamed bar is carved from solid rock and the room is decorated with old photos, prints and brasses and has an open fire. You can play dominoes, cribbage, darts, shove ha'penny and table skittles.

School House, Low Marishes, *Yorkshire*

Never a school, the isolated whitewashed and porched pub is in a tiny agricultural community on the banks of the River Derwent, standing on land reclaimed from Lake Pickering. Landlord Jim Bell has decked out the pub with air force memorabilia and enamel jugs; he stages an annual real ale festival with beers from every small Yorkshire brewery free from the clutches of the commercial giants.

Birch Hall Inn, Beck Hole, *Yorkshire*

There is a timeless air to this lovely old inn in a peaceful village with a steep road, tucked into the moors close to where Eller Beck and West Beck meet to form the Esk. The pub was once two cottages and is the focal point of the village, acting as the post office and sweet shop as well as the meeting place for the lively quoits team. The exterior has whitewashed rough stone walls with an ancient painting of the nearby Thomason Fosse waterfall as outside decoration. Inside beer and sandwiches are served through a hatch into the simply furnished bar. Side steps take you up into a small garden with delightful views across the moors. As well as the waterfall, the village is close to the North Yorks Moors steam railway. You can walk along a disused track to Goathland.

Greyhound
Saxton, *Yorkshire*

The Greyhound has a magnificent setting next to a Norman church in an ancient village close to Tadcaster. You enter the whitewashed exterior of the pub through an impressive porch. Inside the floors are stone-flagged and the tap room is a masterpiece, its timeless air underscored by a coal-burning fire, ochre coloured walls, a cushioned window seat and an etched glass window that looks into a tiny snug used by the village cricket team in the summer. Down the corridor, another room is a haven for pub games, offering darts, shove ha'penny, table skittles, cribbage, dominoes and cards. In season the exterior of the Greyhound is a riot of bright flowers and there are picnic tables in a side courtyard. Just north of the village is the site of the Battle of Towton, 1461, the bloodiest battle in the protracted Wars of the Roses; Lord Dacre, a Lancastrian who died during it, has a monument to his memory in the village church-yard.

Malt Shovel
Oswaldkirk, *Yorkshire*

The village is mentioned in the Domesday Book; its inn dates from 1610 when it was the local manor house. It is a back-to-front building, not especially striking from the road but with a fine façade overlooking lovely gardens that include a box-hedge maze. Inside there is another maze – of ancient wood-panelled rooms. The tap room is superb with its old wooden settles and low beams, a rocking armchair, old clay pipes and miners' lamps. A family room has a vast inglenook fireplace, and the lounge is half wood-panelled with beams and a small stone fireplace. The seventeenth-century wooden staircase is yet another fine feature of the pub. The thirteenth-century church in this hillside village is where Archbishop Tillotson, pioneer of modern English, first preached in 1661.

Farmers Arms, Muker, *Yorkshire*

The pub in the centre of this old riverside Swaledale village lives up to its name for it is first and foremost a farmers' pub created from two cottages in the seventeenth century. Muker was once the centre of the lead-mining industry with a population of 1500. It is now down to just seventy souls but still manages to support a brass band. Be warned though: both the writer's and photographer's cars broke down here.

George Inn, Hubberholme, *Yorkshire*

That no-nonsense, pipe-smoking archetypal Yorkshireman, J. B. Priestley, is buried in the churchyard across the bridge from the George; of all the Dales pubs he knew, the George was his favourite. Hubberholme, which consists of church, bridge, a few houses and the inn, is named after the Viking king Hubba who settled in the area. The road through the Dales village is the highest in Yorkshire, reaching 1,934 feet.

Eastern England

It was rumoured that when Mr Webster . . . left the Maid's Head, the whole scope of the old house – the nearest approach to the typical old hostel that I ever saw – was going to be changed; that it was going to be let to a big brewer, and turned into a commercial inn, with a coloured glass bar, a billiard-room, and the rest of it; in fact, that the whole place was to be spoiled, and no longer a refuge for those who like peace and quiet and old surroundings.

— WALTER RYE, THE MAID'S HEAD, NORWICH

ALL THE PUBS OF BRITAIN OWE A GREAT DEBT TO EAST ANGLIA, FOR IT IS the major barley-growing region of the country. The fine varieties of maritime barley are ideal for brewing and the ripe, fruity ales of Norfolk, Suffolk and the adjoining counties pay homage to a cereal that brewers call 'the soul of beer'. The region was once a brewing powerhouse but the number of breweries declined as if in step with the general decline of the region itself. It was once a major wool and weaving area, dominated by Norwich and influenced by generations of Flemish immigrants who added new inflections to the gentle and quizzical local dialect.

The medieval town of Lavenham, rich in half-timbered houses, is testimony to the wealth of the weavers of old. Suffolk in particular has many beautiful old villages while such small coastal towns and villages as Southwold and Walberswick were once important harbours until the rivers were silted up. Dunwich, the most important ancient harbour town of all and seat of religious power, is now just a tiny speck on the coast, most of the town having fallen into the sea over the centuries. The ceaseless pounding of the waves along the

Norfolk and Suffolk coast is caught majestically in the sea music of Benjamin Britten, born in Lowestoft and founder of the Aldeburgh Festival. Framlingham, a medieval military town, retains some of its castle; close by are some small wine makers who prove that this part of England can be hot and sunny. Much of Ipswich's history has been lost by thoughtless town planners but Norwich remains a fine, workaday city with a soaring cathedral watched over by the squat Norman castle. The heart of Cambridge is the university, founded in 1284 by the Bishop of Ely, and made up today of a fascinating clash and complement of buildings, from the timber-framed lodge at Queen's College to the brick and stone grandeur of Trinity.

From the fens came Hereward the Wake, who almost defeated the Normans at Ely, and Oliver Cromwell of Huntingdon, who was rather more successful in seeing off the divine right of kings. Essex, a county split between its rural areas and the outer suburbs of London, has history a-plenty in Colchester, England's oldest town; a Roman garrison destroyed by Boudicca, it now boasts the remains of a Norman castle, some Georgian houses and a splendid Victorian town hall.

Brewing is slowly reviving in the region. Cambridgeshire and Hertfordshire have just one commercial brewer each and Essex has two. But Suffolk has several new micros to add to the pleasures provided by such famous names as Adnams, Greene King and Tolly Cobbold. Norfolk lost all its breweries when the giants went on the rampage in the 1960s and 1970s, but now Woodforde's and the smaller Reepham are supplying beers of great distinction.

PREVIOUS PAGE **Cap and Feathers**, Tillingham, *Essex (see page 154)*
OPPOSITE **The Bell**, Walberswick, *Suffolk (see page 154)*

Queen's Head
Newton, *Cambridgeshire*

This seventeenth-century converted farmhouse has been popular with monarchs. Anne of Cleves is the queen in question on the pub sign, though she has no known connection with the pub. Before the outbreak of hostilities in 1914, King George and the German Kaiser enjoyed a drop here and the Shah of Iran and his wife had lunch in the pub before he lost the Peacock Throne. The dark brick-faced building with its impressive tall chimney stands at the junction of five roads close to Cambridge and was once a major coaching inn. The quality of the farmhouse beer encouraged the owner to turn it into an ale house for the general public. It has not changed much over the centuries: the main bar has bow windows, a curved high-back settle and scrubbed benches, a yellow tiled floor, seats in the fireplace and a loudly ticking clock. A corridor off the main bar leads to a small room where you can play such fascinating old pub games as devil among the tailors – a version of table skittles – and nine men's morris, an Elizabethan board game.

Butt and Oyster
Pin Mill, *Suffolk*

The tiny riverside hamlet of Pin Mill is a place of pilgrimage for lovers of Arthur Ransome's children's novels: both hamlet and pub feature in *We Didn't Mean To Go To Sea*. The Orwell, which gave a pen name to another famous writer, is dotted with yachts and great sailing barges: at low tide you can stroll down the causeway and get a different perspective on the seventeenth-century whitewashed inn. The main bar, with its enormous bowed window, has views across the river to the wooded shore on the other side; at high tide the water laps just below the window. The bar has flagstoned floors, high-backed settles, an open log fire and wood-panelled walls decorated by model sailing ships, old photos and tobacco advertisements. A long and polished serving counter runs at a right angle to the dominant window; it has a ship's engine indicator at one end with the handle on Stop. The best thing about the Butt is that it is a pub used primarily by the sailors who earn their living on the Orwell.

King's Head, Laxfield, *Suffolk*

Don't ask for the King's Head for this thatched Tudor pub is known to all and sundry as the Low House. It is not a house of ill-repute; the name stems from the fact that it lies in a dip below the churchyard and down the slope from Laxfield's other pub. Its free-standing pub sign is not certain which monarch it is celebrating; one side shows Henry VIII, the other Charles I.

The doorway leads into a simple parlour dominated by a great three-sided, high-backed settle that faces an open fire. The space behind the settle is a passageway with wall seats. Beer is drawn straight from casks kept in a back room (*right*). A room near the beer store has a table and chairs and is popular with locals who want to play cribbage and dominoes. Laxfield, a medieval wool-town, has a half-timbered guildhall and the church has a memorial to William 'Smasher' Downing, Puritan destroyer of church ornaments.

Cock
Brent Eleigh, *Suffolk*

You reach the Cock through superb countryside, the fringes of Constable Country, with gently rolling fields and village after village of ancient half-timbered houses. The pub is known locally as 'Sam Potter's Cock', after the retired landlord who ran the place for years and who still drops in for a pint and a chat most days. The exterior is barley white with a thatched roof and has two dormers nestling under the eaves, topped by two tall chimneys.

Inside it is very simple: a small snug and a larger bar with a single table and a darts board. In winter fires blaze in two hearths, while both rooms are served by a single bar. There is nothing so modern as a handpump and ale is brought from casks stillaged at the back. The locals play darts and other pub games and will attempt to engage you in conversation in an incomprehensible version of the 'Suffuk' dialect. Learn the language and join in.

Cat and Mouse
Wetheringsett, *Suffolk*

This is a pub for animal lovers, with donkeys, goats, rabbits, dogs, ducks and geese and a vast army of cats. No mice, though. One of the cats is called Wadworth after a famous real ale from Wiltshire, which sets the tone of a pub with a vast range of beers served from casks behind the bar, and there are good local ciders too. The pub is plain and simple outside, with whitewashed walls, a few hanging baskets and a small beer garden. Inside there are three rooms with perilously low ceilings. The tiny bar to the left was once the parlour of the cottage before it became a pub. It has low beams, a flagstoned floor and a tiled fireplace, with a clock on the mantel. Old photos of the area cover the whitewashed walls. The larger central bar has many knick-knacks on the cat-and-mouse theme. The third room leads off the bar and has comfortable armchairs, standard lamps and a wood-burning stove. It's simple, comfortable and welcoming.

The Hill House
Happisburgh, *Norfolk*

You approach Happisburgh – pronounced Hazeboro – across flat countryside, guided by the tall tower of St Mary the Virgin and a red-and-white striped lighthouse: the village is named after a dangerous sandbank off the coast. The pub, dating from 1710, has an imposing red-tiled and dormered roof above rough whitewashed walls with black-painted windows. Inside the cheerful locals' bar has a framed collection of beer bottle labels. The pub was popular with Sir Arthur Conan Doyle, who wrote some of his Sherlock Holmes stories here, though Happisburgh is a far cry from foggy Baker Street.

Lifeboat
Thornham, *Norfolk*

The Lifeboat is a sixteenth-century smugglers' inn on the edge of the salt marshes running down to the sea: the smugglers used to bring contraband, such as French brandy, tobacco and silk, across the marshes to the lonely inn. Today doves coo peacefully in a converted beer cask in the car park and cows graze in the surrounding fields. The Lifeboat is a rambling white-faced building almost certainly converted from several cottages. The main bar has a low beamed ceiling with suspended oil lamps, tiled floor, chunky oak tables, old wooden settles, and pews and reed slashers and other agricultural tools.

Pub games include darts, shove ha'penny and dominoes and the rare penny-in-a-hole, built into an old wooden bench (*right*). To play you have to throw thirteen old coins against a lead backdrop and get them to pitch into the hole where they are caught in a tray underneath. Winners – who are rare – may claim a gallon of whisky.

Lord Nelson
Burnham Thorpe, *Norfolk*

England's most famous sea dog was born in Burnham Thorpe and learned his nautical skills along the Norfolk coast. The pub named in his honour fêtes him in style. This simple old ale house is a celebration of the life and times of the admiral, with sixty prints dedicated to his exploits and an old ship's bell hanging from an enclosed beam in the bar. Landlord Leslie Winter is punctilious about using the right term for the pub: 'It is an ale house, not a tavern,' he says. The reason is that the Lord Nelson, with its high-backed settles and flagstoned floor, concentrates on serving good ale straight from casks tapped in a back room.

Mr Winter is a dedicated enemy of nicotine. On the day he banned the weed he half-cleaned a picture of HMS Victory that hangs in the bar. The cleaned glass gives a good view of the ship, the rest is still a murky yellow-brown, a potent warning to addicts.

Brocket Arms
Ayot St Lawrence
Hertfordshire

For a tiny village Ayot St Lawrence
has a lot to offer: the home of George
Bernard Shaw, the ivy-girt ruins of a
medieval church and its striking
Palladian successor and the
fourteenth-century pub that is
owned by members of the
aristocratic Brocket family; their
Hall is just down the road. The pub is
white-walled with a steeply pitched
roof. Inside the two bars are
untouched by time, with low beams
and lanterns, wall settles and a vast
inglenook fireplace. Darts and
dominoes flourish and locals tend to
arrive on horseback as well as by car
and foot for the pub's good range of
ales and cider. With a ruined church
only a few yards away it is not
surprising that the pub is haunted by
a monk.

Chequers
Thompson, *Norfolk*

Chequers, represented by one of the
oldest inn signs, is a fitting name for
this ancient ale house that is more
than 400 years old. Its steeply raked
thatched roof hangs so low to the
ground that two small dormer
windows look like eyes. You have to
crouch low to enter what was once
several small cottages. A long bar
serves the interconnected rooms
with their exposed wall beams, a
wood-burning stove and old
wheelback chairs. The walls are
covered with old farming tools and
copper and brass artefacts. Close by
is Griston Hall where the most
famous wicked uncle of all is said to
have dumped the Babes in the
Wood.

THE FOX & HOUNDS

Fox and Hounds, Barley, *Hertfordshire*

The village with a name redolent of beer and brewing is close to the Cambridgeshire border, a juxtaposition which stresses that you are now firmly in the grain belt of Eastern England. The Fox and Hounds is a higgledy-piggledy building, precariously topped by a tall chimney. It has one of the few surviving examples of a 'gallows' inn sign stretching across the road; this one shows hounds in full cry after a fox. Such signs were all the rage centuries ago when landlords built ever more extravagant signs to attract passing trade.

The low-ceilinged building has been a pub since 1797 and before that was used by James I as a lodge when he was hunting in the Royston area. Inside it is a warren of small rooms with log fires either side of a massive central chimney. It is a sports-mad pub, being the meeting place of the local cricket and football teams and providing facilities for darts, dominoes, bar billiards and shove ha'penny.

Thames Valley and Cotswolds

Whoe'er has travell'd life's dull round,
Where'er his stages may have been,
May sigh to think he still has found
The warmest welcome, at an inn.
– WILLIAM SHENSTONE, *at an Inn in Henley*

THE THAMES VALLEY HAS MANY ATTRIBUTES, INCLUDING 'THE BEST BEER in England' according to playwright John Mortimer who lives locally. Henley, famous for its regatta, seems rather too snooty to have a brewery but Brakspear's elegant buildings fit in well. In common with many older breweries, it was built alongside a river to receive supplies of malt and hops and to send its beers out by barge. Brakspear's, its founder distantly related to England's only Pope, Nicholas Breakspear, was one of the first country breweries to establish good trade in London. But their wonderfully ripe and hoppy beers are best enjoyed in ancient Chiltern and Cotswold ale houses among beechwood trees and gentle hills.

Oxford dominates the region and remains a magnificent city despite its terrible traffic problems. Close at hand is the charming town of Woodstock, adjacent to Blenheim Palace, birthplace of Winston Churchill. Oxfordshire has done well to keep several breweries intact. The capital has Morrells, maintaining a medieval tradition of university colleges being supplied with ale by their own brewers, Abingdon has Morland while Hook Norton has a brewery of the same name with a clutch of simple old ale houses.

The Cotswolds can be bleak in winter but when the sun shines it seems an area

of unparalleled peace and tranquillity, if it were not for the fighter planes confronting mythical enemies in the skies above. Villages with names such as Shipton-under-Wychwood are filled with delightful houses and cottages of honey-stone brick. Burford by the River Windrush, gateway to the Cotswolds, is perhaps the most famous of all preserved small towns while close by Kelmscott Manor was the country home of designer, artist and utopian socialist William Morris. The village of Great Tew has rows of seventeenth- and eighteenth-century thatched and iron stone cottages with a village green and stocks. The local lords of the manor allowed the village to fall into delapidation but now it has been lovingly restored, and the re-opened Falkland Arms pub is its focal point.

Berkshire and Buckinghamshire have suffered badly from brewery closures. The axing of the much-loved Wethered's brewery in Marlow rankles still and, be warned, beers that carry the Wethered name are brewed a long way from their original source. Buckinghamshire has two tiny micro breweries while Berkshire has only a national brewer's processed beer factory. The two counties have strong Civil War connections and many fine villages with the old tradition of houses and pubs set round the village green.

PREVIOUS PAGE **Falkland Arms**, Great Tew, *Oxfordshire (see page 154)*
OPPOSITE **Bell**, Waltham St Lawrence, *Berkshire (see page 154)*

Old Crown
Skirmett, *Buckinghamshire*

The name is picked out in the tiny gable above the entrance to this 350-year-old pub tucked away near the Oxfordshire border. It was once three separate cottages (one of which used to be the village shop) and is whitewashed and gabled. Inside there is a wealth of old beams, and logs burn in the large inglenook fireplace on cold days. The white-painted tap room is superb with a quarry-tiled floor, trestle tables and an ancient settle by the coal fire. Beer comes straight from the cask and is served through a hatch. The walls of the pub are crowded with some seven hundred pieces of bric-à-brac, including paintings, plates, bottles and tools. There's a cheerful Alsatian dog called Bruno and in summer you can sit in the garden at the back or among the flower tubs on the sheltered front terrace and watch the cows in the field opposite.

Bull and Butcher
Turville, *Buckinghamshire*

The black-and-white timbered cottage pub lies in a wooded and serene Chilterns valley by the village green and old church. A windmill that stands on the hill behind the village featured in the film 'Chitty Chitty Bang Bang', and the motor car theme is echoed in the pub where there are many old photos of racing cars: a previous owner was a racing-driver. There are two low-ceilinged bars with cushioned wall settles and a high-backed settle by a log fire. There's a locals' cards and dice school one evening in the week and the pub also offers darts, dominoes and cribbage. You will be forced to drink Brakspear's Henley ales and farm cider is also available. If you go during the week when the pub is not crowded you may catch old Charlie, in checked shirt and cloth cap, propping up the bar: he cleans the pumps and will be happy to talk about the pub, the village and the excellence of the ale.

Chequers
Fingest, *Buckinghamshire*

The Chequers has a brick-and-flint, white-shuttered exterior and stands in a delightful village overlooking the Hambleden Valley and opposite St Bartholomew's church which has a unique twin-roofed Norman tower. The central bar of the pub has ceiling beams, a log fire, an eighteenth-century settle and wall seats. It is decorated with Toby jugs, pewter mugs, decorative plates, pistols, old guns and swords. A sun-filled lounge has comfortable chairs and french windows leading into the large garden. You can play backgammon, cribbage and dominoes, and Brakspear's ale from Henley is sublime. The pub is in good walking country and is popular all year round with orienteers. Henley and the Thames are some eight miles away.

Bell, Aldworth, *Berkshire*

The geese waddling on the forecourt sum up the rural charm of this ancient ale house dating back to the fifteenth century. It started life as a manor hall and it retains an impressive creeper-covered exterior with a fine porched entrance. Ian Macaulay, the present landlord, is a phlegmatic, pipe-smoking presence in the hatched servery; his wife's family has run the pub for some 200 years. The beamed tap room has benches built round the walls and in the gaps left by a disused fireplace and bread oven; a wood-burning stove remains and watch out for the one-handed clock. The garden is sublime, ablaze with roses and lavender in season. Morris Dancers underscore the pub's bucolic charm with their occasional performances, and at Christmas mummers perform in the road outside by the ancient village well head and jugs of punch and hot mince pies are dispensed. The Bell won the accolade of British Pub of the Year in 1991 from CAMRA.

The Pear Tree
Hook Norton, *Oxfordshire*

The red-brick, three-storey Pear Tree stands out boldly in an isolated village with cottages of Cotswold stone and a brewery that bears the same name of Hook Norton. The pub has a fine porched entrance and creepers clambering up the walls. The two small bars have been knocked into one, to the annoyance of some regulars, but there is still a lot of unfussy charm, comfortable furnishings, a warm fire in winter and a large garden to enjoy in summer.

The brewery has two other pubs in the village but the Pear Tree is the most popular with locals, so follow the small but knowledgeable crowd. The beer is immaculate as it should

be with the brewery just a hundred yards away. It is a classic Victorian 'tower' brewery where the brewing process flows simply and logically from top to ground floor. Watch out for the strong Old Hooky ale: if you sample too much you may have to stay the night.

Handpumps are the most recognizable sign that a pub serves real ale. When pulled, the handle operates a simple suction pump that draws beer through a pipe from the cask in the pub cellar. But many village pubs were built without cellars and publicans stillage their beers on the ground floor and draw the beer straight from the casks.

Hop Country and the Downs

A tavern is a degree or (if you will) a pair of stairs above an ale-house . . . it is the busy man's recreation, the idle man's business, the melancholy man's sanctuary, the stranger's welcome, the Inns of Court man's entertainment, the scholar's kindness, and the citizen's courtesy.

— JOHN EARLE, 1628

THIS IS THE GARDEN OF ENGLAND, NO HIGH MOUNTAINS OR DEEP LAKES but acre after acre of gently undulating countryside with fine soil that encourages extensive orchards. Fruit comes in abundance here, along with an odd little plant that has an important part to play in the taste and the history of beer. Hops arrived in Kent in the early part of the fifteenth century; they had been used for centuries in mainland Europe to add bitterness to beer but the British had doggedly stuck with their stronger and sweeter ales. Dutch and Flemish merchants introduced hopped beer and the art of hop cultivation into the Winchelsea area in 1400. The plant, which grows wild if not carefully controlled, is a member of the same family as the nettle and cannabis, and contains oils and resins that give the characteristic peppery, resiny aroma and taste to beer.

Kent supplies ninety per cent of the hops used by British brewers, and the landscape is criss-crossed by the tall poles and trellises up which the plants climb and dotted with the oast houses with their wonky cowls in which the hops are dried. English hop growing was in the doldrums for years as a result of the rise of imitation European lager-style beers in Britain but traditional ale is now making a spirited comeback and hops are once more in demand. The county town,

Canterbury, has its world-famous cathedral while Dover and its white cliffs is equally famous as the major port of entry from France and Belgium. The region has some superb villages, many with thatched and timbered cottages.

In Sussex Brighton is a bright and breezy seaside resort while its more sedate neighbour, Hastings, is considered to be the scene of the battle in 1066 where the Normans defeated the English; it actually took place a few miles away where the village of Battle now stands. Castles and squat Martello towers, built to watch out for the invading French, stand sentinel along the region's coastline. The flat sands of the Romney Marsh include several of the Cinque Ports developed as part of the anti-French barricades. Rye and Winchelsea, two of the ports, have scarcely changed for centuries and feature some stunning timbered buildings, including Rye's great inn, the Mermaid.

Surrey, before it expires into the London suburbs, has the cathedral and university city of Guildford, such Betjeman-derided towns as Camberley and some surprisingly untouched old villages and inns. The county has lost all its commercial breweries and is represented now by just one micro in Reigate. Sussex has fared a little better with two long-standing independents, including Harvey's of Lewes, its splendid Victorian 'tower' brew house standing alongside the river. Kent, despite being the heart of the hop country, has been devastated by closures and has just one large commercial brewery, Shepherd Neame, in the market town of Faversham, and two tiny micros.

PREVIOUS PAGE **Castle**, Chiddingstone, *Kent* (*see page 154*)
OPPOSITE **The Volunteer**, Sutton Abinger, *Surrey* (*see page 154*)

Three Chimneys, Biddenden, *Kent*

The first thing you notice about this early sixteenth-century pub is that it has just two chimneys. The name has nothing to do with smoke stacks but is a corruption of the French 'trois chemins'. During the Seven Years War with France in the middle of the eighteenth century, French prisoners-of-war were kept at nearby Sissinghurst Castle. They were permitted to take country walks but could go no further than the junction of three roads – *les trois chemins* – where the pub stands.

The whitewashed and half-timbered Three Chimneys seems to have changed little since that trade war between Britain and France. It is a warren of small rooms with low beams, wood-panelled walls and flagstoned floors. The tiny public bar, where locals congregate, is dominated by a vast inglenook. The beamed ceiling forces most visitors to stoop to reach the bar, which is carved from solid timber.

The Mounted Rifleman, Luddenham, *Kent*

This plain old ale house almost lost down country lanes a few miles from Faversham is the complete antithesis of the low-beams-and-inglenook inn. It stands well back from the lane in the hamlet of Elverdon: Luddenham is the nearest place on the map. The entrance is a side door above which is the inscription 'Tomson & Wotton 1634 Old Brewery' which conveniently dates the place.

The pub has two half-panelled rooms with oil cloth on the floor; the main room has a darts board, an open fire and a few benches and chairs. The smaller room has a serving area with hop bines above the hatch; behind the hatch is a kitchen table, sink and Aga cooker. There is no bar as such, for Bob Jarrett the landlord goes down to the cellar and brings back glasses of beer for his customers. Bob was born in the pub, which has been run by his parents, grandparents and possibly even his great-grandparents.

Red Lion
Snargate, *Kent*

Doris Jemison is one of that small but doughty group of matriarch landladies that provide welcome change in a male-dominated pub trade. The Red Lion has been in her family's hands since 1911 and she has no intention of letting it go, a fact emphasized by her position in front of the bar where she knits away like a *tricoteuse* awaiting the tumbrils. The white-painted building is four hundred and fifty years old and was last 'modernized' in 1890. It has two simple but homely bars, one of which is used as a family room. The boards are bare and the walls wood-panelled. Good ale and cider are drawn from casks – a bank of fine pewter and brass handpumps are just ornaments.

The pub is a veritable museum of traditional pub games: you can play bat and trap, skittles, bar billiards, shove ha'penny and toad in the hole, which really is a game and not a meal: it is a variation of penny in the hole in which coins or small weights are thrown into a hole in a pub seat or into a small box or cabinet.

Three Horseshoes, Elsted, *Sussex*

This cattle drovers' inn dating from Tudor times looks, with its several entrances, as though it was once two cottages that became one: a regular event when the ale brewed by one household became so popular that it was sold commercially and bigger premises were needed. The Three Horseshoes sells local eggs to help out hard-pressed chicken farmers and it is a place of pilgrimage for lovers of traditional pub pastimes such as the dice game shut-the-box, dominoes and cribbage. The exterior is cheerfully whitewashed with a steep tiled roof and a mass of creepers and flowers. Inside the small connecting rooms have stone fireplaces, low beams, ancient settles and benches. The rustic charm is underscored by candlelight in the evening and the walls are covered with fascinating old prints and photos. The booze is spectacular: up to ten ales from independent breweries are tapped straight from the cask.

The Bull
Ticehurst, *Sussex*

The full and appealing address is The Bull, Three Legged Cross. The curious name arose centuries ago when there was a hangman's gibbet near the pub. The Bull is fourteenth-century and is a rambling red-bricked building set in fine gardens with fruit trees and a weeping willow by a pond. The heart of the pub is the original bar with its large central fireplace – popular with the pub cat – and heavy oak tables. A more modern room has areas for darts, dominoes and cribbage.

Scarlett Arms
Walliswood, *Surrey*

Or is it the Scarlet Arms? The name on the whitewashed pub has two 'ts' but there is only one on the free-standing inn sign. The red-tiled building was once two labourers' cottages as can be seen from the two front doors, one of them with a handsome porch. The cottages date from 1620 and the interiors have been lovingly preserved. The three connecting rooms have blackened beams holding up the nicotine-stained ceiling, polished flagstoned floors, wooden trestles and benches and cheering log fires, one in a large inglenook. One room is set aside for darts, dominoes and cribbage. In summer visitors can enjoy the fine views from the attractive garden.

Crown
Chiddingfold, *Surrey*

Here is history by the cart-load. The Crown is seven hundred years old and is at its most delightful in high summer, its exterior covered by laburnum, lilac and wisteria. Edward VI was a frequent visitor but he will have been less impressed with the thick stone walls, open fires, inglenooks and great central chimney, which were run-of-the-mill for the aristocracy in his time but now send a shiver of antiquity down the back.

You need more than a quick pint to take in all the splendours. The oak beams are more than two feet thick, there is magnificent carving around the inglenook fireplace, some splendid oak panels and a coin collection some four hundred years old found during renovation work. Marvel at the stained-glass windows – the crests are those of local villages – and sit in a sedan chair that has been converted into an unusual phone box. In fine weather you can sit in the garden or courtyard and stroll round the village with a church of similar age to the pub's.

Photographer's Notes

A REALLY GOOD VILLAGE PUB OFTEN DEPENDS ON A COMBINATION OF different factors, for example, the beer, the company you are with, the food, the scenery, the weather, and of course your mood. Different things for different people. I have tried, and I hope succeeded, in creating a mood in the pictures that works without any of these elements, except the weather. All our village pubs are photographed without people except for a few characters. There are no cars, no 'No Parking' signs, no sun umbrellas, no dirty ash trays, no waste paper baskets and few benches and tables.

Before I started on this project I drank gin and tonic or an occasional Guinness. At lunch I drank Appletise. Thirteen thousand miles later and after visiting well over one hundred and fifty village pubs I have been converted. I'm a Real Ale enthusiast now.

In the course of working on this book I travelled throughout England. It's a wonderful country, full of unspoilt beautiful villages set in an exquisite and diverse landscape. The journey from The Farmers Arms in Muker, over the Pennine Way to Tan Hill, and on to The Rose and Crown in Romaldkirk is really quite stunningly beautiful, with the most wonderful dramatic light glancing off dark irregular stone walls that create a varied patchwork of steep hill fields. A visual experience never to be forgotten.

All the photographs were taken on Nikon cameras. A 28mm and 35mm lens for the wider shots and interiors; a 80–200mm zoom lens for the exterior shots. Cokin graduated filters were usually used in conjunction with 81 B and C warm up filters. The interiors were carefully constructed and lit with Elinchron, Multiblitz and Norman lighting systems. An exposure of between ½ a second and a 15th of a second was normal. I made use of as much ambient light as possible to 'fill' the dark corners and to give a more natural feel to the pictures. Kodachrome 64 professional film was used. It's a high quality medium speed film that I found ideal for this job.

I never left home without a compass so that I could check where the light would be coming from at any particular time of the day. Tall step ladders and a heavy tripod were used to gain height and stability for the exterior shots while I waited for the light to change, and the cars and people to move on. The wait was often four or five hours and occasionally even longer. Numerous pubs were visited twice. One interesting and beautiful pub in the North York Moors I visited on four occasions without taking a single picture. I was finally beaten by the licensee's daughter's blue Ford that she had left parked outide. She had gone to work sixty miles away that day with a friend and she had taken her car keys with her. There were no spare keys! I drove home.

Of course I didn't discover all the village pubs. Roger with his expertise and intimate knowledge as an aleologist furnished me with a very long list. I would like to thank him for providing such an illuminating selection. I would like to thank all the landlords and landladies and their helpers who gave me access, without whose co-operation I would not have been able to work. Finally I would like to say 'thank you' to Emma my editor who had the forethought and faith in my ability which made this experience possible.

HOMER SYKES
JANUARY 1992

ACKNOWLEDGEMENTS

THANKS TO ALL THE LANDLORDS AND LANDLADIES WHO GAVE GENEROUSLY of their time to answer a barrage of questions about their pubs and who found that visits were followed by letters and frantic phone calls as the book's deadline approached. Their splendid devotion augurs well for the survival of the British pub. Thanks, too, to members of the Campaign for Real Ale, the British Guild of Beer Writers and brewers for suggesting pubs for inclusion in the book. And finally and as always devoted thanks to my wife, Diana, for once again letting me go to the pub. R.P.

OPPOSITE **The Crown Inn**, St Ewe, *Cornwall* (see also page 21)

Tuckers Grave, Faulkland, *Somerset*

The curious name of the pub derives from the suicide in 1747 of Edward Tucker, who hanged himself from a beam in the farm barn.

Miners Arms, Mithian, *Cornwall*

The Miners Arms dates from 1577: the back bar has bulging walls, a beamed ceiling, wood-block floor and a wall painting of Elizabeth I. Bare stone walls and uncovered floors abound and the age of the pub is underscored by a once-secret passage to the local manor house and a penance cupboard where wrongdoers were incarcerated.

Compasses, Chicksgrove, *Wiltshire*

There is a wonderful timeless air of peace and tranquillity inside, with bare brick walls decorated with farm tackle, low beamed ceilings, partly flagstoned floors and settles dividing the single room into many quiet and secluded alcoves.

Hurdlers Arms, Binley, *Hampshire*

This small red-brick ale house was first used by rural craftsmen who built the hurdles or moveable fences used to pen sheep and other animals. The pub is more than three hundred years old and was mentioned in William Cobbett's *Rural Rides*.

Boat Inn, Ashleworth Quay, *Gloucestershire*

The Boat, lies on the banks of the River Severn and is an unspoilt fifteenth-century red-brick cottage pub. It has been run for as long as anyone can remember by Irene Jelf and her niece. The pub is simply two small parlour rooms where you are made welcome by the two women.

Royal Oak, Whatcote, *Warwickshire*

This particular Royal Oak was used by the head of the Commonwealth as temporary quarters during the battle of Edge Hill in 1642. The bread oven was removed to make an observation slit to watch the fighting. The Sealed Knot, fanatical followers of the English Revolution, re-enact the battle in the pub gardens every October.

Red House, Knipton, *Leicestershire*

The three-storeyed, red-brick Georgian building is a former hunting lodge in a delightful village in the Vale of Belvoir. Part of the estate of the Duke of Rutland, the terms of the lease are that it must act as an inn for the estate staff from Belvoir Castle and the 'hunt servants'.

Rose and Crown, Romaldkirk, *Northumberland*

This old coaching inn, is memorably set on the village green, which still has the original stocks. The splendid main bar has a grandfather clock, beams, seats facing a log fire, a Jacobean oak settle, vicious-looking gin traps, farm tools and old photos of Romaldkirk on the walls.

Tower Bank Arms, near Sawrey, *Cumbria*

The pub features in *The Tale of Jemima Puddle-duck* and backs on to Hill Top Farm where Beatrix Potter lived. The Tower Bank Arms, a striking black-and-white building with an impressive porch with a clock built into it, is now owned by the National Trust.

Hare Inn, Scawton, *Yorkshire*

The Hare Inn was built in 1153 by the monks from Old Byland during the construction of Byland Abbey. It has been an ale house and farm and a bit of both over the years and the present lounge used to be a byre. The handpumps that serve the beer are in a cabinet in the original ale house section of the building.

The Bell, Walberswick, *Suffolk*

The tiny village by the sea was a favourite haunt of George Orwell's when he lived in Southwold; he once saw a ghost in the churchyard. The Bell has its own ghost, an old fisherman, while the village is claimed to be haunted by a phantom black dog.

Cap and Feathers, Tillingham, *Essex*

'The Cap' is a splendid example of a white-painted weather-boarded inn. The style is occasionally seen in Kent and parts of East Anglia but it is essentially Essex in character. The pub is a listed building, dates from 1600 and has a twin-gabled roof. It is haunted by a former landlord who was a retired sailor.

Bell, Waltham St Lawrence, *Berkshire*

The sign at this splendid old black-and-white timbered inn is emblazoned below some dramatically curved black beams next to the entrance. Inside the beamed lounge has some superb carved wood panelling, a long-case clock and a good example of an antique oak settle.

Falkland Arms, Great Tew, *Oxfordshire*

For many people, the Falkland Arms is the quintessential English village pub. The fifteenth-century inn is a continuing delight in its magnificent setting among cottages of mellow Cotswold stone and thatch. There is just one room inside the pub with mullioned latticed windows, a great inglenook fireplace and stone-flagged floor worn smooth by the passage of years.

Castle, Chiddingstone, *Kent*

In a village of almost dream-like beauty owned by the National Trust, the pub stands in a row of Tudor cottages and has been the village's essential wateringhole since 1730. An earlier building on the site – Waterslip House – dated from 1420, and it is thought that Anne Boleyn took shelter there once.

The Volunteer, Sutton Abinger, *Surrey*

The pub was used as a recruiting place for the Surrey Yeomanry. The tactic of the recruiting sergeants was to buy villagers drinks and then, unseen, drop coins into their pewter mugs; once the villagers had touched the coins they were deemed to have 'kissed the sovereign' and could not refuse military service. Hatred of the tactic is thought to have hastened the switch from pewter to glass drinking vessels.

BIBLIOGRAPHY

The Good Beer Guide (CAMRA, published annually).

The Good Pub Guide (Ebury Press, published annually).

The Best Pubs in Devon and Cornwall, The Best Pubs in East Anglia, The Best Pubs in Lakeland, The Best Pubs in Yorkshire (all Alma Books/CAMRA).

CAMRA Guide to Good Pub Food, Susan Nowak (Alma Books).

Classic Country Pubs, Neil Hanson (Pavilion Books/CAMRA).

The Great British Beer Book, Roger Protz (Impact Books).

A Dictionary of Pub Names, Leslie Dunkling and Gordon Wright (Routledge & Kegan Paul).

The Bedside Book of Beer, Barrie Pepper (Alma Books/CAMRA).

The Guinness Book of Pub Games, Arthur Taylor (Penguin).

SELECTED REGIONAL PUB GUIDES PRODUCED BY BRANCHES OF THE CAMPAIGN FOR REAL ALE.

GAZETTEER

Pubs change with time and circumstances so readers are advised to telephone in advance if they plan to visit one of the pubs included in this book.

Abbey Inn, Byland Abbey, Old Byland, N Yorks (034 76) 204
Bell, Aldworth, Berkshire (0635) 578272
Bell, The Street, Waltham St Lawrence, Berkshire (0734) 341788
The Bell, Ferry Road, Walberswick, Suffolk (0502) 723109
Birch Hall Inn, Beck Hole, nr Goathland, N Yorks (0947) 86245
Black Bull, Etal, Northumberland (089 082) 200
Black Horse, Clevedon Lane, Clapton in Gordano, Devon (0272) 842105
Boat Inn, Ashleworth Quay, Ashleworth, Gloucestershire (0452) 70272
Boot, Littledown, nr Vernham Dean, Hampshire (026 487) 213
Brocket Arms, Ayot St Lawrence, Hertfordshire (0438) 820250
The Bull, Three Legged Cross, Ticehurst, Sussex (0580) 200586
Bull and Butcher, Turville, Buckinghamshire (049 163) 283
Bush Inn, Morwenstow, Cornwall (028 883) 242
Butt and Oyster, Pin Mill, nr Chelmondiston, Suffolk (0473) 780764
Cap and Feathers, South Street, Tillingham, Essex (0621) 779212
Case is Altered, Five Ways, Haseley Knob, Warwickshire (0926) 484206
Castle, Chiddingstone, Kent (0892) 870247
Cat and Mouse, Pages Green, Wetherup Street, Wetheringsett, Suffolk (0728) 860765
Chequers, Fingest, Buckinghamshire (049 163) 335
Chequers, Griston Road, Thompson, Norfolk (0953) 83360
Cock, Brent Eleigh, nr Lavenham, Suffolk (0787) 247407
Compasses, Lower Chicksgrove, Wiltshire (072 270) 318
Crook Inn, Tweedsmuir, Border (089 97) 272
Crown, Chiddingfold, Surrey (0428) 792255
Crown, Debdale Hill, Old Dalby, Leicestershire (0664) 823134
Crown Inn, St Ewe, Cornwall (0726) 843322
Drewe Arms, Drewsteignton, Devon

Falcon, Arncliffe, N Yorks (075 677) 205
Falkland Arms, Great Tew, Oxfordshire (060 883) 653
Farmers Arms, Muker, N Yorks (0748) 86297
Fox and Hounds, Barley, Hertfordshire (0763) 848459
George Inn, Hubberholme, N Yorks (075 676) 223
The George Inn, Norton St Philip, Somerset (037 387) 224
Greyhound, Saxton, N Yorks (0937) 817202
Hare Inn, Scawton, N Yorks (0845) 597289
Hill House, The Hill, Happisburgh, Norfolk (0692) 650004
Hole in't Wall, Robinson Place, Bowness-on-Windermere, Cumbria (05394) 43488
Hurdlers Arms, Binley, Hampshire
Jolly Sailor, Lands End Road, Bursledon, Hampshire (0703) 405557
King's Head, Gorhams Mill Lane, Laxfield, Suffolk (0986) 798395
Laurel Inn, Main Street, Robin Hood's Bay, N Yorks (0947) 880400
Lifeboat, Sea Lane, Thornham, Norfolk (048 526) 236
Lord Nelson, Burnham Thorpe, Norfolk (0328) 738241
Malt Shovel, Oswaldkirk, N Yorks (043 93) 461
Martins Arms, Colston Bassett, Nottinghamshire (0949) 81361
Masons Arms, Branscombe (lower village), nr Sidmouth, Devon (029 780) 300
Masons Arms, Strawberry Bank, Cartmel Fell, Cumbria (044 88) 486
Masons Arms, Knowstone, Devon (039 84) 231
Miners Arms, Mithian, St Agnes, Cornwall (087 255) 2375
The Mounted Rifleman, Elvedon, Luddenham, Kent (0795) 522464
Normandy Arms, Blackawton, Devon (080 421) 316
Old Bull, Inkberrow, Hereford & Worcester (0386) 792428
Old Coach House, Ashby St Ledgers, Northamptonshire (0788) 890349
Old Crown, Skirmett, Buckinghamshire (049 163) 435
Olde Gate Inn, Brassington, Derbyshire (062 985) 448

The Pear Tree, Hook Norton, Oxfordshire (0608) 737482

Peter Tavy Inn, Peter Tavy, Devon (0822) 810348

Plough, Wistanstow, Shropshire (0588) 673251

Queen's Head, Newton, Cambridgeshire (0223) 870436

Red House, Knipton, Leicestershire (0476) 870352

Red Lion, Snargate, Kent (0679) 344648

Rhydspence Inn, Whitney-on-Wye, Hereford & Worcester (049 73) 262

Rising Sun, Calstock Road, Gunnislake, Cornwall (0822) 832201

Riverside Inn, Canonbie, Dumfries & Galloway (038 73) 71512

Rock Inn, Haytor Vale, Devon (0364) 6305

Rose and Crown, Romaldkirk, Co. Durham (0833) 50213

Royal Oak, Long Street, Cerne Abbas, Dorset (0300) 341797

Royal Oak, Luxborough, Somerset (0984) 40319

Royal Oak, Whatcote, Warwickshire (0295) 88319

St Kew Inn, St Kew, Bodmin, Cornwall (020 884) 259

Scarlett Arms, Walliswood, Surrey (030 679) 243

School House, Low Marshes, N Yorks (0653) 86247

Square & Compass, Worth Matravers, Dorset (0929) 439229

Star, Melton Lane, West Leake, Nottinghamshire (0509) 852233

Star Inn, Fore Street, St-Just-in-Penwith, Cornwall (0736) 78876

Sun Inn, High Street, Clun, Shropshire (058 84) 277

Sun Inn, Dent, Cumbria (058 75) 208

Three Chimneys, nr Biddenden, Kent (0580) 291472

Three Horseshoes, Elsted, Sussex (0730) 825746

Tibbie Shiels Inn, St Mary's Loch, Border (0750) 42231

Tom Cobley Tavern, Spreyton, Devon (0647 23) 314

Tower Bank Arms, Near Sawrey, Cumbria (096 66) 334

Tuckers Grave, Faulkland, Somerset (0373) 834230

The Volunteer, Sutton Abinger, Surrey (0306) 730798

If you would like to know more about the CAMPAIGN FOR REAL ALE, the address and telephone number are: CAMRA, 34 Alma Road, St Albans, Hertfordshire AL1 3BW; (0727) 867201.

INDEX